Contents

Brazil 1

China 4

India 10

Russia 14

South Africa 20

Brazil

Eduardo Soares
Senior Foreign Law Specialist

SUMMARY   In Brazil, the violation of trade secrets is considered crime of unfair competition and is regulated by Law No. 9,279 of May 14, 1996. A constitutional principle protects the confidentiality of the source when necessary for the performance of a professional activity. For civil remedies, the Civil Code determines that a person who practices an illicit act and causes damage to another person is obligated to repair the damage caused. The Code of Civil Procedure allows for the search and seizure of a person or thing provided that the requester justifies the reasons for the measure, and Brazilian Labor Law grants employers the right to terminate an employee for violation of a trade secret.

I. Industrial Property Law

In Brazil, Law No. 9,279 of May 14, 1996, regulates rights and duties related to industrial property. According to article 195(XI), whoever reveals, exploits, or uses, without authorization, knowledge, information, or confidential data used in industry, commerce, or services to which the person has had access through a contractual or employment relationship, even after the termination of the contract or relationship, commits the crime of unfair competition, unless the information is public knowledge or obvious to someone with the required technical skills.[1]

It is also considered a crime of unfair competition to reveal, exploit, or use knowledge or information referred to in article 195(XI) of Law No. 9,279 that was obtained by unlawful means or fraud;[2] and to reveal, exploit, or use, without authorization, test results or other undisclosed information that involved a considerable effort and has been presented to government agencies as a condition for the approval of products for commercialization.[3]

Employers, partners, or officers of a company are also subject to prosecution for those crimes described in articles 195(XI) and 195(XII) of Law No. 9,279.[4] When necessary to protect the public, however, the provisions of section XIV of article 195 of Law No. 9,279 do not apply to the disclosure of information by a government agency responsible for authorizing the commercialization of the product.[5]

In the event that confidential information, such as industrial secrets or trade secrets, is revealed in court for the defense of the interests of any party, the judge must order that the trial be

---

[1] Lei No. 9.279, de 14 de Maio de 1996, art. 195(XI), http://www.planalto.gov.br/ccivil_03/Leis/L9279.htm.

[2] *Id.* art. 195(XII).

[3] *Id.* art. 195(XIV).

[4] *Id.* art. 195(§1).

[5] *Id.* art. 195(§2).

continued in private.[6] The use of such information is forbidden and the other party may not use it for any other purpose.[7]

Regardless of any criminal actions, the aggrieved party may file applicable civil actions pursuant to the terms of the Code of Civil Procedure.[8] Compensation is determined according to the benefits that the injured party would have received if the violation had not occurred.[9]

The law guarantees the injured party the right to ask for compensation for loss and damage caused by the infringement of industrial property rights and unfair competition not provided for in Law No. 9,279 that may cause harm to the reputation or business of others, create confusion among commercial or industrial establishments or service providers, or create confusion between the products and services available in commerce.[10]

II. Constitutional Principle

Article 5(XIV) of the Brazilian Constitution states that access to information is assured to everyone and the confidentiality of the source is protected when necessary for the performance of a professional activity.[11]

III. Civil Code

Pursuant to article 229(I) of the Civil Code, no one may be obligated to testify regarding facts which, by his status or profession, the person must keep secret.[12]

With regard to illicit acts, the Civil Code determines that a person who, by a voluntary act or omission, negligence, or imprudence, violates the rights of and causes damage to another, even though the damage is exclusively moral, commits an illicit act.[13]

A person who practices an illicit act (articles 186 and 187 of the Civil Code) and causes damage to other persons is obligated to repair the damage.[14] The employer or principal is also responsible for the civil damages caused by his employees, servants, and agents in the

---

[6] *Id.* art. 206.

[7] *Id.*

[8] *Id.* art. 207.

[9] *Id.* art. 208.

[10] *Id.* art. 209.

[11] CONSTITUIÇÃO FEDERAL art. 5(XIV), http://www.planalto.gov.br/ccivil_03/Constituicao/Constituicao.htm.

[12] CÓDIGO CIVIL, Lei No. 10.406, de Janeiro de 2002, art. 229(I), http://www.planalto.gov.br/ccivil_03/Leis/2002/L10406.htm.

[13] *Id.* art. 186.

[14] *Id.* art. 927.

performance of their work or because of it.[15] The amount of compensation is measured by the extent of the damage.[16]

IV. Code of Civil Procedure

Like the Civil Code, the Code of Civil Procedure also protects trade secrets by stating that a party is not obligated to testify about facts that, by status or profession, the person should keep secret.[17] Parties and witnesses may be excused from showing in court a document or thing if its exhibition entails the disclosure of facts about which, by status or profession, they should keep secret.[18]

As for legal remedies the Code states that a judge may order the search and seizure of persons or things.[19] In the request for the search and seizure the requester must state the reasons that justify the measure and the knowledge that the person or thing is in the designated place.[20] If necessary, this justification for the search and seizure can be made in private.

Once the allegations are proved, the search and seizure warrant is issued. The warrant must indicate the house or place where the warrant is to be served, describe the person or thing sought, designate what should be done with the person or thing, and be signed by the judge who issued the order.[21]

V. Labor Law

According to article 482 of the Brazilian Consolidation of Labor Laws, a violation of trade secrets constitutes just cause for termination of employment by the employer.[22]

---

[15] *Id.* art. 932(III).

[16] *Id.* art. 944.

[17] CÓDIGO DE PROCESSO CIVIL, Lei No. 5.869, de 11 de Janeiro de 1973, art. 347(II), http://www.planalto.gov.br/ccivil_03/Leis/L5869compilada.htm.

[18] *Id.* art. 363(IV).

[19] *Id.* art. 839.

[20] *Id.* art. 840.

[21] *Id.* art. 841.

[22] CONSOLIDAÇÃO DAS LEIS DO TRABALHO, Decreto-Lei No. 5.452, de 1 de Maio de 1943, art. 482(g), http://www.planalto.gov.br/ccivil_03/Decreto-Lei/Del5452.htm.

China

Laney Zhang
Foreign Law Specialist

SUMMARY   In China, the enforcement of trade secret protection may include criminal prosecution under the Criminal Law and administrative penalties under the Anti-Unfair Competition Law. The Anti-Unfair Competition Law also provides for compensatory damages as civil remedies to the trade secret owner, as do other civil and commercial laws such as the Contract Law and Labor Contract Law. A preliminary injunction for trade secret misappropriation used to be unusual, but this may be changing.

I. Introduction

This report summarizes China's legal regime for enforcing trade secret protection and the civil remedies provided for trade secret owners to combat misappropriation. Trade secrets were first addressed by the Civil Procedure Law enacted in 1991, which briefly mentioned the protection of trade secrets in civil proceedings.[1]

The primary trade secret regulations are provided by the 1993 Law on Anti-Unfair Competition (Anti-Unfair Competition Law). Under the Law, misappropriation of trade secrets may be punished by administrative penalties. The Law also provides for compensatory damages as civil remedies to the trade secret owners.[2]

Later, when the Criminal Law was revised in 1997, misappropriation of trade secrets was written into the new Law as a crime. Persons who commit such an offense may be subject to imprisonment for up to seven years. In terms of civil law, although trade secrets are not addressed by the General Principles of the Civil Law, the protection of trade secrets and remedies for the owner may be found in individual civil and commercial laws, including the Contract Law, Labor Law, Labor Contract Law, and Company Law.

II. Criminal Law

A misappropriation of trade secrets that causes serious losses to the owner may constitute a crime under the Criminal Law. According to article 219 of the Criminal Law, whoever commits any of the prescribed acts and thus causes "serious losses" to a trade secret owner will be punished by a fine, or a fine and up to three years' imprisonment or criminal detention. When

---

[1] 中华人民共和国民事诉讼法 [Civil Procedure Law] (promulgated and effective Apr. 9, 1991), arts. 66 & 120, *available at* WESTLAWCHINA (by subscription).

[2] 中华人民共和国反不正当竞争法 [Anti-Unfair Competition Law] (promulgated Sept. 2, 1993, effective Dec. 1, 1993), *in* 新编中华人民共和国常用法律法规全书 [NEW COMPLETE FREQUENTLY-USED LAWS AND REGULATIONS OF THE PEOPLE'S REPUBLIC OF CHINA] 4-352 (2012).

the losses are "exceptionally serious," the violator will be sentenced to imprisonment of three to seven years and a fine. The prescribed acts include any of the following:

(1) Acquiring a trade secret of another by theft, inducement, duress, or other illegal means;

(2) Disclosing, using, or allowing others to use a trade secret of another acquired by the above illegal means;

(3) Disclosing, using, or allowing others to use a trade secret in breach of an agreement or a confidentiality obligation imposed by a legal owner; or

(4) Acquiring, using, or disclosing a trade secret by a third party, when he knew or should have known that the trade secret has been misappropriated in any of the aforementioned ways.[3]

The Supreme People's Court has issued a judicial interpretation that sets forth the specific thresholds for determining whether losses are "serious" or "exceptionally serious." According to the interpretation, losses over 500,000 yuan (about US$80,000) are "serious losses," while losses over 2,500,000 yuan are "exceptionally serious losses."[4]

Criminal prosecution is "always" considered by lawyers practicing in China as an enforcement option when the trade secret owner has suffered great losses, "because police in China have the power to seize any relevant evidence, which can also be used in administrative or civil litigation."[5]

III. Anti-Unfair Competition Law

The Anti-Unfair Competition Law is the primary statute in the current Chinese legal system providing protection for trade secrets. The Law defines those trade secrets that deserve legal protection, the acts that may be deemed as misappropriation of trade secrets, and the legal liabilities for misappropriation including administrative penalties and civil liabilities.

In 2007, the Supreme People's Court issued a judicial interpretation on the application of the Anti-Unfair Competition Law (Judicial Interpretation), which provides for more detailed rules regarding trade secret protection under the Anti-Unfair Competition Law.[6]

---

[3] 中华人民共和国刑法 [Criminal Law] (promulgated July 1, 1979, revised Mar. 14, 1997, effective Oct. 1, 1997, last amended Feb. 25, 2011), art. 219, in NEW COMPLETE FREQUENTLY-USED LAWS AND REGULATIONS OF THE PEOPLE'S REPUBLIC OF CHINA 6-1 to 6-46 (2012).

[4] 最高人民法院、最高人民检察院关于办理侵犯知识产权刑事案件具体应用法律若干问题的解释 [Interpretation of the Supreme People's Court & the Supreme People's Procuratorate Concerning Some Issues on the Specific Application of Law for Handling Criminal Cases of Infringement upon Intellectual Property Rights] (promulgated Dec. 8, 2004, effective Dec. 22, 2004, Fa Shi [2004] No. 19), art. 7, available at WESTLAWCHINA.

[5] J. Benjamin Bai & Guoping Da, *Strategies for Trade Secrets Protection in China*, 9 NW. J. TECH. & INTELL. PROP. 351, 364 (2011).

[6] 最高人民法院关于审理不正当竞争民事案件应用法律若干问题的解释 [Interpretation of Supreme People's Court on Some Issues Concerning the Application of Law in the Trial of Civil Cases Involving Unfair Competition], (Fa Shi [2007] No. 2, issued Jan. 12, 2007, effective Feb. 1, 2007), available at WESTLAWCHINA.

A. Definition of Trade Secrets

According to article 10 of the Anti-Unfair Competition Law, "trade secrets" are defined as technical or business operation information that

- is unknown to the public,
- can bring economic benefits to the owner,
- has practical utility, and
- for which the trade secret owner has adopted measures to maintain its confidentiality.[7]

The Judicial Interpretation provides definitions of the terms "unknown to the public," "can bring economic benefits to the owner and has practical utility," and "confidentiality measures" under article 10 of the Anti-Unfair Competition Law.[8] The Interpretation specifically allows acquiring trade secrets through "independent creation" and reverse engineering, which are not deemed a misappropriation of trade secrets under the Anti-Unfair Competition Law. The Interpretation also provides a definition of "customer lists."[9]

B. Misappropriation of Trade Secrets

Under the Anti-Unfair Competition Law "misappropriation of trade secrets" includes

- acquiring the trade secret of another by theft, inducement, duress, or other illegal means;
- disclosing, using, or allowing others to use the trade secret of another acquired by the above illegal means; or
- disclosing, using, or allowing others to use a trade secret in breach of an agreement or a confidentiality obligation imposed by a legal owner.[10]

According to the Judicial Interpretation, a plaintiff who claims that a defendant has misappropriated its trade secret bears the burden of proving that its trade secret meets the statutory requirements, that what the defendant uses is similar or substantially similar to its trade secret, and that the defendant has used illegal means.[11]

---

[7] Anti-Unfair Competition Law art. 10.

[8] Judicial Interpretation arts. 9–11.

[9] *Id.* arts. 12 & 13.

[10] *Id.* art. 10.

[11] *Id.* art. 14. *See also* Bai & Da, *supra* note 5.

C. Administrative Penalties

The administrative enforcement of trade secret misappropriation is within the authority of the offices of the Administration for Industry and Commerce (AICs) above the county level.[12] Article 17 of the Anti-Unfair Competition Law prescribes the authorities AICs may have in overseeing and investigating trade secret misappropriation cases.[13]

After the investigation and determination of misappropriation, the AICs may order the cessation of the illegal acts and impose a fine of not less than 10,000 yuan (about US$1,600) but not more than 200,000 yuan.[14] The AICs may further order the return of drawings, blueprints, and other materials containing the trade secrets, and the destruction of goods manufactured using the stolen trade secrets, if such goods would disclose the trade secrets to the public when made available.[15]

D. Civil Remedies

1. Compensatory Damages

An aggrieved owner of a trade secret may seek compensatory damages under the Anti-Unfair Competition Law. According to article 20 of the Law, any business operator who violates the provisions of this Law and thus causes damage to the infringed business operators must bear the liability of compensation for the damage.[16] When losses of the trade secret owner are difficult to determine, the court may award damages in the same amount as the profits derived from the misappropriation.[17]

To seek compensatory damages, a trade secret owner must file a lawsuit. The government authorities imposing administrative penalties are not authorized to award compensatory damages, although the authority may act as a mediator in the negotiation upon the request of the trade secret owner.[18]

2. Injunctions

In the past it was unusual to obtain a preliminary injunction for trade secret misappropriation in China, although when the plaintiff prevails in a trade secret misappropriation case, the court may order the cessation of the illegal acts for a period of time until the trade secret becomes known to the public, or for another period which the court believes reasonable.[19]

---

[12] 国家工商行政管理局关于禁止侵犯商业秘密行为的若干规定 [Several Provisions on Prohibiting Infringements upon Trade Secrets] (issued Dec. 3 1998), art. 4, http://gkml.saic.gov.cn/auto3743/auto3746/200807/ t20080729_112473.htm.

[13] Anti-Unfair Competition Law art. 17.

[14] *Id.*

[15] Several Provisions on Prohibiting Infringements upon Trade Secrets art. 7.

[16] Anti-Unfair Competition Law art. 20.

[17] *Id.*

[18] Several Provisions on Prohibiting Infringements upon Trade Secrets art. 9.

[19] Judicial Interpretation art. 16. *See also* Bai & Da, *supra* note 5, at 361.

A recent court order indicates that the past reluctance to issue injunctions in trade secret cases may be changing. On August 2, 2013, Shanghai No. 1 Intermediate Court granted a preliminary injunction in a trade secret misappropriation case involving an American plaintiff. This was widely reported in the domestic media as the first trade secret preliminary injunction order made in accordance with article 100 of the newly amended Civil Procedure Law.[20]

Indeed, the order is significant because the court clearly cited to article 100, which is the article on property preservation and injunctions.[21] Previously, it appeared to be unclear whether a preliminary injunction could be ordered in accordance with this article in trade secret cases. Injunctions may be expected to be ordered more frequently in these cases if other courts adopt similar approaches.

IV. Protection and Civil Remedies Under Other Laws

A. Contract Law

Under the Contract Law, if a party discloses or inappropriately uses a trade secret obtained while negotiating a contract and such a disclosure or use causes loss to the other party, the party is responsible for compensatory damages regardless of whether the contract was actually executed.[22]

Protection of technological know-how is addressed in the chapter of the Contract Law regulating technology transfer. Under that chapter, the licensor and licensee of technological know-how may stipulate the scope of the use of the technological know-how in a technology licensing agreement, provided that no restriction may be imposed on technological competition and development.[23]

The licensee of a technology transfer contract must undertake confidentiality obligations with regard to the secret parts of the technology provided by the licensor in accordance with the scope and for the time period agreed upon in the contract.[24]

---

[20] 上海一中院发出国内首个商业秘密行为禁令 [*Shanghai No. 1 Intermediate Court Issued Nationwide First Trade Secret Injunction Order*], *in* 新民晚报 (Aug. 6, 2013), *available at* http://news.xinhuanet.com/fortune/2013-08/06/c_116833932.htm.

[21] Article 100 of the Civil Procedure Law provides that, "[i]n the cases where the execution of a judgment may become impossible or difficult or otherwise harmful to the parties concerned because of the acts of one party or for other reasons, the people's court may, at the application of the other party, make a ruling to preserve the assets of the other party or order the other party to perform certain acts or to prohibit the other party from committing certain acts; where no application is filed by either party, the people's court may also rule to take preservation measures when it deems necessary." Civil Procedure Law (as amended Oct. 28, 2007, effective Apr. 1, 2008) art. 100, *in* NEW COMPLETE FREQUENTLY-USED LAWS AND REGULATIONS OF THE PEOPLE'S REPUBLIC OF CHINA 7-19 (2012).

[22] 中华人民共和国合同法 [Contract Law of the P.R.C.] (promulgated Mar. 15, 1999, effective Oct. 1,1999), art. 43, *in* NEW COMPLETE FREQUENTLY-USED LAWS AND REGULATIONS OF THE PEOPLE'S REPUBLIC OF CHINA 2-83 (2012).

[23] *Id.* art. 343.

[24] *Id.* art. 350.

A licensee who uses a trade secret in a manner that exceeds the agreed scope or unilaterally permits a third party to use the trade secret in violation of the contract will be ordered to cease the act and will be liable for breach of contract. A party violating the agreed confidentiality obligations is also liable for breach of contract.[25]

B. Labor Law and Labor Contract Law

The 1995 Labor Law provides that parties to a labor contract can enter into a confidentiality agreement regarding the employer's trade secrets in a labor contract.[26] If an employee breaches a labor contract in violating the confidentiality agreement and causes losses to the employer, the employee is liable for compensatory damages.[27]

The 2008 Labor Contract Law also provides that employers may impose confidentiality obligations regarding the employer's trade secrets and other intellectual property on employees in a labor contract.[28] For an employee who bears the obligation to keep the employer's trade secrets, the employer may stipulate competition restrictions in the labor contract or confidentiality agreement, and the payment of financial compensation to him on a monthly basis during the term of the competition restriction after the labor contract is revoked or terminated. If the employee breaches the stipulation on competition restriction, he must pay damages to the employer as agreed upon by the parties.[29]

C. Company Law

The Company Law prohibits directors or managers of a company from illegally disclosing the company's secrets.[30] The Law further provides that if directors or managers violate the law, regulations, or the company's articles of incorporation during the course of employment and cause harm to the company, they must be liable for damages.[31]

---

[25] *Id.* arts. 351 & 352. *See also* Bai & Da, *supra* note 5.

[26] 中华人民共和国劳动法 [Labor Law] (promulgated July 5, 1994, amended Aug. 27, 2009), art. 22, *in* New Complete Frequently-Used Laws and Regulations of the People's Republic of China 5-90 (2012).

[27] *Id.* art. 102. *See also* Bai & Da, *supra* note 5.

[28] 中华人民共和国劳动合同法 [Labor Contract Law] (promulgated Jun 29, 2007, effective Jan. 1, 2008), art. 23, *in* NEW COMPLETE FREQUENTLY-USED LAWS AND REGULATIONS OF THE PEOPLE'S REPUBLIC OF CHINA 5-97 (2012). *See also* Bai & Da, *supra* note 5.

[29] *Id.*

[30] 中华人民共和国公司法 [Company Law] (promulgated Dec. 29, 1993, last amended Oct. 27, 2005, effective June 1, 2006), art. 149, *in* NEW COMPLETE FREQUENTLY-USED LAWS AND REGULATIONS OF THE PEOPLE'S REPUBLIC OF CHINA 2-132 (2012).

[31] *Id.* art. 150.

India

Tariq Ahmad
Legal Research Analyst

SUMMARY | There is no specific legislation that regulates trade secrets in India. The courts have protected trade secrets through common law actions for breach of confidence or breach of contract. In the absence a contract, Indian courts have also relied on the principle of equity to provide protection in some instances. Civil remedies include damages, injunctions, and the return of the confidential information.

I. Protection of Trade Secrets

Currently there is no specific or separate legislation that regulates the protection of trade secrets and confidential information in India.[1] However, the courts in India have relied on equitable and common law remedies as a means of protecting trade secrets. Specifically, Indian courts have relied on the principles laid out in the *Saltman Engineering* case,[2] which, as summarized by Patrick Hearn, author of *The Business of Industrial Licensing*, states that

> . . . maintenance of secrecy, according to the circumstances in any given case, either rests on the principles of equity, that is to say the application by the court of the need for conscientiousness in the course of conduct, or by the common law action for breach of confidence, which is in effect a breach of contract.[3]

In other words, "[i]n India, parties must primarily rely on contracts to protect trade secrets."[4] However, "Indian law does recognize the common law tort of 'breach of confidence' irrespective of the existence of a contract."[5] According to a New Delhi Court, a trade secret "can be a formulae, technical know-how or a peculiar mode or method of business adopted by an employer which is unknown to others."[6] However, the Court adds that, "routine day-to-day affairs of employer which are in the knowledge of many and are commonly known to others cannot be

---

[1] Zafar Mahfood Rahmani & Faizanur Rahman, *Intellection of Trade Secret and Innovation Laws in India*, 16(4) J. INTELL. PROP. RTS. 341, 347 (July 2011), http://nopr.niscair.res.in/bitstream/123456789/12449/1/IJPR%2016%284%29%20341-350.pdf.

[2] Saltman Engineering Co. Ltd. v. Campbell Engineering Co. Ltd., 1948 (65) R.P.C. 203.

[3] PATRICK HEARN, THE BUSINESS OF INDUSTRIAL LICENSING: A PRACTICAL GUIDE TO PATENTS, KNOW-HOW, TRADE MARKS, AND INDUSTRIAL DESIGN 112 (1986), *quoted in* John Richard Brady and Others v. Chemical Process Equipments P. Ltd. and Another, A.I.R. 1987 Delhi 372.

[4] Sonia Baldia, *Offshoring to India: Are Your Trade Secrets and Confidential Information Adequately Protected?*, MAYER BROWN BUS. & TECH. SOURCING REV., Mar. 1, 2008, at 10, http://www.mayerbrown.com/files/Publication/c4321838-f2ec-4fe5-990d-1ea497a7398b/Presentation/PublicationAttachment/5a87579c-8d2b-469d-ad3d-bb95435fe6ff/ART_OFFSHORINGTOINDIA_0308.PDF.

[5] *Id.*

[6] Ambiance India Pvt. Ltd. v. Shri Naveen Jain, 122 (2005) D.L.T. 421, para. 6.; *see also* American Express Bank, Ltd. v. Priya Puri, (2006) 3 L.L.N. 217.

called trade secrets."[7] The requirements for a cause of action for a breach of confidence that are used by the Indian courts are borrowed from the English common law and are enunciated as follows:

> (1) the information itself must have the necessary quality of confidence about it;
>
> (2) that information must have been imparted in circumstances imparting an obligation of confidence;
>
> (3) there must be an unauthorized use of that information to the detriment of the party communicating it.[8]

Moreover, the Indian Courts have applied these principles in three sets of circumstances out of which proceedings may arise:

> (a) Where an employee comes into possession of secret and confidential information in the normal course of his work, and either carelessly or deliberately passes that information to an unauthorized person;
>
> (b) Where an unauthorized person (such as a new employer) incites such an employee to provide him with such confidential information . . . ; and
>
> (c) Where, under a license for the use of know-how, a licensee is in breach of a condition, either expressed in any agreement or implied from conduct, to maintain secrecy in respect of such know-how and fails to do so.[9]

Many trade secret decisions come in the context of breach of contract proceedings for restraint of trade. The courts have held that, "although an employer is not entitled to restrain his servant after the termination of employment from offering competition, he is entitled to reasonable protection against exploitation of trade secrets."[10] Moreover, absent a contract, courts in India have still issued injunctions based on the rules of equity.[11]

II. Available Remedies

In India only civil or equitable remedies are available for a breach of confidence cause of action. The available remedies include the award of an injunction "preventing a third party from disclosing the trade secrets," the return of all "confidential and proprietary information," and compensation or damages "for any losses suffered due to disclosure of trade secrets."[12] The court may also order the party at fault to "deliver-up" such materials.[13]

---

[7] Ambiance India Pvt. Ltd. v. Shri Naveen Jain, para. 6.

[8] Emergent Genetics India Pvt. Ltd. v. Shailendra Shivam and Ors., (2011) 125 D.R.J. 173, para. 33.

[9] Homag India Private Ltd. v. Mr. Ulfath Ali Khan (Oct. 2012), http://judgmenthck.kar.nic.in/judgments/bitstream/123456789/759406/1/MFA1682-10-10-10-2012.pdf (quoting the Delhi High Court in John Richard Brady and Others v. Chemical Process Equipments P. Ltd. and Another, A.I.R. 1987 Delhi 372).

[10] Rahmani & Rahman, *supra* note 1, at 346.

[11] John Richard Brady and Ors. v. Chemical Process Equipments P. Ltd. and Anr., A.I.R. 1987 Delhi 372.

[12] DEEPAK GOGIA, CHAKRAVARTY'S INTELLECTUAL PROPERTY LAW 753 (2010).

[13] PARAMESWARAN NARAYANAN, INTELLECTUAL PROPERTY LAW 331 (1990).

Injunctions may be interlocutory (interim relief) or permanent. According to Advocate P. Narayanan, "[t]he information may remain confidential only for a limited period in which case the injunction will not extend beyond that period."[14] Moreover, "[s]ince the information alleged to be confidential may be of value to the plaintiff only for a specified period, interim injunction will ordinarily be granted only for a specified period depending upon the circumstances and the nature of the confidential information."[15] The rules that the courts use to determine whether to award an interim or permanent injunction were summarized as follows in the *Gujarat Bottling Co. Ltd.* case:

> The grant of an interlocutory injunction during the pendency of legal proceedings is a matter requiring the exercise of discretion of the Court. While exercising the discretion the Court applies the following tests – (i) whether the plaintiff has a prima facie case, (ii) whether the balance of convenience is in favour of the plaintiff, and (iii) whether the plaintiff would suffer an irreparable injury if his prayer for interlocutory injunction is disallowed. The decision whether or not to grant an interlocutory injunction has to be taken at a time when the existence of the legal right assailed by the plaintiff and its alleged violation are both contested and uncertain and remain uncertain till they are established at the trial on evidence. Relief by way of interlocutory injunction is granted to mitigate the risk of injustice to the plaintiff during the period before that uncertainty could be resolved. The object of the interlocutory injunction is to protect the plaintiff against injury by violation of his right for which he could not be adequately compensated in damages recoverable in the action if the uncertainty were resolved in his favour at the trial. The need for such protection has, however, to be weighed against the corresponding need of the defendant to be protected against injury resulting from his having been prevented from exercising his own legal rights for which he could not be adequately compensated. The Court must weigh one need against another and determine where the "balance of convenience" lies.[16]

The determination of damages is based on the "market value of the confidential information based on a notional sale between a willing seller and a willing purchaser."[17]

III. Proposed Legislation

In 2008, the Department of Science and Technology, as part of the Ministry of Science and Technology, published draft legislation titled the National Innovation Act of 2008[18] that would in part "codify and consolidate the law of confidentiality in aid of protecting Confidential Information, trade secrets and Innovation."[19] Trade secrets would be regulated under Chapter

---

[14] *Id.*

[15] *Id.*

[16] Gujarat Bottling Co. Ltd. v. Coca Cola Co., (1995) 5 S.C.C. 545, para. 43.

[17] NARAYANAN, *supra* note 13, at 42.

[18] National Innovation Act of 2008 (Bill), http://www.dst.gov.in/draftinnovationlaw.pdf.

[19] *Id.*, preamble.

VI, which is titled "Confidentiality and Confidential Information and Remedies and Offences."[20] The current status of this draft legislation is unclear.

---

[20] *Id.* ch. VI.

Russian Federation

Peter Roudik
Director of Legal Research[*]

SUMMARY   General civil law principles apply equally to the protection of trade (commercial) and production (know-how) secrets. Legal protection extends to information that was formally classified as secret and to cases when the owner of the secrets took the measures required to protect them. In cases where protected secrets are divulged, violators are subject to civil, criminal, administrative, and disciplinary measures. Civil remedies are usually limited to direct real damages incurred as the result of the trade secret infringement. Injunction relief can be requested by the owner of the information in order to prevent further damage.

I. Introduction

In general, the protection of trade secrets[1] and the trade secrecy regime with respect to information comprising production secrets (know-how) is provided in the Civil Code of the Russian Federation,[2] particularly Part IV, which deals with intellectual property objects.[3] Some specific areas of trade secrecy protection are regulated by individual federal acts, such as the Federal Law of the Russian Federation on Trade Secrets,[4] the Labor Code of the Russian Federation,[5] and other laws and regulations that relate to different aspects of trade and production secrets, including measures of civil protection and remedies for breach of the trade secrecy regime.

---

[*] This report was prepared with the assistance of the Law Library intern Svitlana Vodyanyk.

[1] In Russian legislation the phrase *kommercheskaia tayna* is used to mean "trade secret" or "commercial secret," with most of the existing translations of Russian legal sources into English translating the phrase as "commercial secret."

[2] GRAZHDANSKII KODEKS ROSSIISKOI FEDERATSII [CIVIL CODE OF THE RUSSIAN FEDERATION], SOBRANIE ZAKONODATEL'STVA ROSSIISKOI FEDERATSII [SZ RF] [Collection of Russian Federation Legislation] (official gazette) 1996, No. 5, Item 410, *available at* http://base.garant.ru/10164072/ (in Russian).

[3] *Id.* Part IV, SZ RF 2006, No. 52(1), Item 5496, *available at* www.rupto.ru/rupto/nfile/3b05468f-4b25-11e1-36f8-9c8e9921_fb2c/Civil_Code.pdf (in English).

[4] Federal'nyi Zakon Rossiiskoi Federatsii o Kommercheskoi Taine [Federal Law of the Russian Federation on Trade Secrets], SZ RF 2004, No. 32, Item 3283, *available at* http://base.consultant.ru/cons/cgi/online.cgi?req=doc;base=LAW;n=116684 (in Russian).

[5] TRUDOVOI KODEKS ROSSIISKOI FEDERATSII [LABOR CODE OF THE RUSSIAN FEDERATION], SZ RF 2002, No. 1(1), Item 3, *available at* http://www.ilo.org/dyn/natlex/docs/WEBTEXT/60535/65252/E01RUS01.htm (in English).

II. Protection of Trade Secrets Under Russian Legislation

Russian legislation defines two types of secrets that receive the same level of protection: trade secrets and production secrets,[6] and while "the legal rules might seem sketchy,"[7] such secrets are protected from

- insiders to whom the secrets have been entrusted,
- outsiders who obtain the secrets by improper means, and
- government agencies that might obtain and release the secrets.[8]

The Civil Code defines "production secret" as information of any type (production, technological, economic, organizational, etc.) that is not generally known, to which the general public does not have open access, and with respect to which the owner of such information has instituted the regime of trade secrecy.[9] Such information could relate to the results of intellectual activity in the areas of science and technology and the methods for carrying out any professional activity having real or potential commercial value.[10]

At the same time, the Federal Law on Trade Secrets (Trade Secrets Law) extends the regime of trade secrecy to information comprising production secrets.[11] However, some Russian scholars have argued that the legal concepts of "production secret" and "trade secret" are not the same in that they play two completely different roles in the process of production and sales, and that a trade secret may consist of much broader information than a production secret.[12]

In order to receive full legal protection, the measures aimed at preserving secrecy must meet minimum requirements established by the Trade Secrets Law. The owner must define the scope of the trade secret, identify the sources of the information to be protected, implement procedures for access to and utilization of this information, and maintain control over the people who have access to the information.[13] If these requirements are not met, the information might not get protection in court should it be divulged. For example, in a case adjudicated by a district court in one of the Russian provinces in 2011, the plaintiff filed an unjust enrichment lawsuit against the defendant, a limited liability company, claiming that the defendant misappropriated his trade secrets. The court dismissed the claim because the plaintiff had not instituted a secrecy regime

---

[6] D.M. Betrov, *Trade Secrets and Production Secrets: New Aspects of Legislation*, VESTNIK URFO, 2011, No. 2, at 13, *available at* http://elibrary.ru/item.asp?id=17321314 (in Russian).

[7] THE REVIVAL OF PRIVATE LAW IN CENTRAL AND EASTERN EUROPE: ESSAYS IN HONOR OF F.J. FELDBRUGGE 387 (George Ginsburgs, Donald D. Barry & William B. Simmons eds., The Hague, 1996).

[8] *Id.*

[9] CIVIL CODE art. 1465.

[10] *Id.*

[11] Federal Law on Trade Secrets art. 3(1).

[12] Betrov, *supra* note 6, at 14.

[13] Artem Sirota, *On Contributing Know-How in Capital of Russian Company*, RUSSIAN LAW ONLINE, http://www.russianlawonline.com/content/contributing-know-how-capital-russian-company (last visited Aug. 8, 2013).

against third parties with respect to his trade secrets and, therefore, this information could be considered as "generally known."[14]

Russian law does not state what information can be classified as a trade secret. It is up to the court to decide whether to qualify certain information as a protected trade secret or generally known information that may not enjoy legal protection.[15]

III. Liability for Violating the Rights of Trade Secret Owners

The Civil Code and Trade Secrets Law provide the general principles and types of liability for infringing exclusive production rights and/or trade secrets. The Trade Secrets Law states that violating the rights of trade secret owners entails disciplinary, civil, administrative, or criminal liability as provided by legislation.[16] Statutory civil remedies include damages incurred as a result of the trade secret infringement.[17] Other types of remedies may be established by a contract or other legislative act.[18] Russian case law specifies that public legal entities, including constituent components of the Russian Federation and municipalities, are liable for the infringement of trade secrets as any other individual or legal entity, if the officials of such public entities who had access to the trade secrets unlawfully disclosed these secrets to third parties.[19]

A. General Measures of Civil Protection

General principles of civil liability for violating the exclusive rights of the owners of intellectual property, including trade and production secrets, are established by the Civil Code. The Code states that enforcement of these exclusive rights must be exercised by putting forward a claim

- for the recognition of the right – against the person who denies or in another manner does not recognize the right, thereby infringing the interests of the right holder;

- seeking injunctive relief (preventing the actions that infringe the right or create a threat of infringement) – against the person taking such actions or preparing to take them;

- seeking damages – against the person who has unlawfully used a result of intellectual activity or means of individualization without the conclusion of an agreement with the right holder

---

[14] Mikhail Zinkovsky, *If an Employee Misappropriated Production Secrets (Know-How): The Five Most Pressing Issues*, TRUDOVYE SPORY, 2011, No. 12, at 40–50, *available at* http://mazinkovsky.ru/sekrety-proizvodstva (in Russian; last visited Aug. 8, 2013).

[15] *Id.*

[16] Federal Law on Trade Secrets art. 14.

[17] CIVIL CODE art. 1472.

[18] *Id.*

[19] Joint Resolution of the Plenary Sessions of the Supreme Court of the Russian Federation No. 5 and of the Supreme Arbitration Court of the Russian Federation No. 29 on Selected Issues Related to the Implementation of Part IV of the Russian Federation Civil Code, Mar. 26, 2009, ROSSIISKAIA GAZETA [ROS. GAZ.] (official publication) No. 70, Apr. 22, 2009, *available at* http://base.consultant.ru/cons/cgi/online.cgi?req=doc;base=LAW;n=86879 (in Russian).

(noncontracted use), or has infringed his exclusive right in another manner and has inflicted damage on him;

- for seizure of the physical carrier – against its producer, importer, depositor, carrier, seller, other distributor, or bad faith buyer; and

- for publication of the judicial decision on the infringement committed with an indication of the actual right holder – against the infringer of the exclusive right.[20]

B. Payment of Damages

Unlawful access to and misappropriation of trade secrets give rise to civil liability because of harm caused. In this case, all general provisions on civil remedies for harm are applied.[21] The following provisions of the Civil Code appear to be applicable in such instances:

- Harm caused to the property of an individual or a legal person is subject to compensation in full by the person who has caused the harm.[22]

- A law or contract may provide for the duty of the offender to pay compensation to the victim in excess of the compensation for harm.[23]

- A person who has caused harm will be released from compensating for harm if he proves that the harm was not caused through a fault of his own. A law may also provide for compensation for harm in the absence of the offender's fault.[24]

- A legal person is to compensate for the harm caused by its employee while performing his or her professional duties.[25]

- When satisfying a claim for compensation for harm, the court must consider circumstances and obligate the person responsible for causing the harm to compensate for the harm in kind or compensate for the losses incurred.[26]

The remedies are limited to direct real damages incurred as the result of the trade secret infringement.[27] The burden of proof of trade secret protectability and of the unlawfulness of the infringer's actions rests upon the plaintiff.[28]

---

[20] CIVIL CODE art. 1252.

[21] Eduard Gavrilov, *Commentaries on the Federal Law on Trade Secrets*, ZONA ZAKONA.RU, http://www.zonazakona.ru/law/comments/159/ (in Russian; last visited Aug. 8, 2013).

[22] CIVIL CODE art. 1064.1.

[23] *Id.*

[24] *Id.*

[25] *Id.* art. 1068.1.

[26] *Id.* art. 1082.

[27] Sirota, *supra* note 13.

[28] M. Rylskaya, *Liability for Violating the Rights of the Owner of a Trade Secret*, TRANSPORTNOE DELO ROSSII, 2011, No. 12, at 106, *available at* http://elibrary.ru/item.asp?id=19052220 (in Russian; last visited Aug. 8, 2013).

C. Injunctive Relief

The owner of a trade secret can require an offender to restore the situation that existed before the violation of the rights and to stop actions that violate the law or may result in the divulging of secrets.[29] Some Russian legal scholars have concluded that this may occur only when the rights of the owner of a trade secret have already been violated but the trade secret itself has not yet been publicly disclosed, i.e., has not lost its ability to be a trade secret.[30]

D. Liability of Employees

Russian law states that an employee who acquired access to information containing a trade secret owing to his or her professional responsibilities upon willful infringement of a trade secret or reckless disregard of secrecy protection measures is subject to disciplinary liability in accordance with the existing legislation,[31] which may include a warning, reprimand, or dismissal.[32]

According to one Russian attorney, "Russian labor law is not flexible enough to ensure effective protection which foreign investors may expect."[33] The financial liability of employees for trade secret infringement is limited to direct actual damages incurred.[34] This may include losses sustained by an employer as a result of the reduction of his personal property or the deterioration of such property's condition, as well as expenditures or excess payments by the employer that became necessary in order to purchase the property, restore the property, or compensate for the damage inflicted by the employee on third persons.[35] The loss of profits caused by the infringement of trade secrets by an employee cannot be recovered.[36] Usually, the financial liability of employees is limited to their average monthly wage, unless otherwise provided by law.[37]

As for the dismissal of an employee for the infringement of trade secrets, Russian case law should be taken into account. The Supreme Court of the Russian Federation has clarified that an employee can be fired for the infringement of commercial secrets if the employer can prove that the disclosed information was classified as a trade secret or other type of secret protected by law,

---

[29] CIVIL CODE art. 1252.

[30] Gavrilov, *supra* note 21.

[31] Federal Law on Trade Secrets art. 14. 2.

[32] LABOR CODE art. 192.

[33] Sirota, *supra* note 13.

[34] LABOR CODE art. 238.

[35] *Id.*

[36] *Id.*

[37] *Id.* art. 242.

that the employee had access to information because of his or her professional activities, and that the employee knew that he or she should not disclose this information.[38]

---

[38] Resolution No. 2 of the Plenary Session of the Supreme Court of the Russian Federation on the Application of the Labor Code of the Russian Federation, Mar. 17, 2004, ROS. GAZ. No. 72, Apr. 8, 2004, *available at* http://base.consultant.ru/cons/cgi/online.cgi?req=doc;base=LAW;n=105228;fld=134;dst=4294967295;rnd=0.37720617139448254;from=65120-0 (in Russian).

South Africa

Hanibal Goitom
*Foreign Law Specialist**

SUMMARY   South Africa does not have specific legislation devoted to protecting trade secrets. However, South Africa's common law protects trade secrets from unauthorized conduct including their acquisition, use, and publication by competitors and current or former employees. South African courts protect information as a trade secret if it meets three requirements: it is capable of application in trade and industry, it is not within public knowledge, and it has an economic value. In cases of infringement of trade secrets, courts can prescribe a number of remedies under contract law and the law of tort (or delict).

I. Introduction

In South Africa, cases involving unauthorized conduct in relation to trade secrets (including acquisition, use, and publication) may be categorized around the actors involved. First, the party involved in the unauthorized conduct may be an employee.[1] In this case, the remedies available to the employer differ depending on whether the violation occurred during or after the termination of the employment contract. Second, the unauthorized use may involve a competitor, which is recognized in South Africa as a form of unlawful competition.[2]

For information to qualify as a trade secret, three requirements must be met: the information must relate to and be capable of application in trade or industry, it must be secret or confidential, and it must be of economic value to the proprietor.[3]

The misappropriation of trade secrets is prima facie wrongful under the laws of South Africa.[4] The existence of a contractual[5] or fiduciary[6] obligation forms a legal basis for the protection of trade secrets and know-how.[7] Over the years South African courts have recognized various forms of information that can be categorized as "confidential," including the following:

---

* This report was prepared with the assistance of Law Library intern Antoinette Ofosu-Kwakye.

[1] VAN HEERDEN-NEETHLING, UNLAWFUL COMPETITION 223 (2d ed. 2008).

[2] *Id.* at 219.

[3] *Id.* at 215. *See also Townsend Production (Pty) Ltd v. Leech* 2001 (4) SA 33 (C).

[4] J. Neethling & B.R. Rutherford, *Competition, in* THE LAWS OF SOUTH AFRICA 195, 267 (L.T.C. Harms & J.A. Faris eds., 2d ed., pt. 2, 2003).

[5] *Reddy v. Siemens Telecommunications* 2007 (2) SA 486, 491, 499–501 (SCA).

[6] *Wespro (Cape Town) v. Stephenson* (1995) 16 ILJ 452, 460–61 (IC), *available at* HeinOnline, http://heinonline.org/HOL/Page?handle=hein.journals/iljuta16&div=50&g_sent=1&collection=journals (by subscription).

[7] *Schultz v. Butt* 1986 (3) SA 667, 678–84 (AD); *see also Strike Productions (Pty) Ltd v. Bon View Trading 131 (Pty) Ltd and Others* (2011), available on the Southern African Legal Information Institute (SAFLII) website, *at* http://www.saflii.org/za/cases/ZAGPJHC/2011/1.rtf.

- Customer lists

- Information received by an employee (or others bound by a fiduciary obligation) regarding business opportunities available to the employer

- Information provided to an employee in confidence during the course of his employment

- Information contained in stolen documents

- Publicly available information when gathered and compiled into a useful form through labor and skill and kept in limited confidence

- Information that relates to the proposal for the name, design, etc., of a new product if it is the result of skill and labor and is kept confidential

- Information on the specifications of a product or manufacturing process obtained through skill and labor and kept confidential

- Tender prices[8]

The confidentiality of any of the above-listed information is not always automatic, absolute, or permanent. Confidential information not classified as a trade secret may be used by an employee for his own benefit or for the benefit of others after the termination of his employment to the extent that it was not copied and/or deliberately memorized for use after termination of the employment contract.[9] For instance, a method for assembling/building a certain machine may be confidential; however, there is a legal recognition that when an employee is terminated from his position, some knowledge acquired during the course of his employment in assembling/building machines will remain in the employee's memory, which he is free to use or distribute, including to a new employer in direct competition with the old one.[10] In addition, confidential information remains confidential for as long as it would take another person to gather such information.[11]

There are instances in which the acquisition, use, and/or publication of trade secrets may not be considered wrongful.[12] Public interest is one justification for waiving the protection that proprietors of trade secrets enjoy.[13] This is particularly true when the issue arises in the context of an employer-employee relationship in which the employee, having acquired certain skills and knowledge by working for one employer, wishes to apply such skills and knowledge in the service of a rival business after termination of the previous employment contract. In this instance, the wrongfulness of the actions of the employee is determined through "the criteria of fairness and honesty" and by weighing the rival interests involved.[14]

---

[8] *Meter Systems Holdings Ltd v. Venter and Another* 1993 (1) SA 409, 410–11 (WLD); *see also* Neethling & Rutherford, *supra* note 4, at 267.

[9] *Strike Productions (Pty) Ltd v. Bon View Trading 131 (Pty) Ltd and Others*, *supra* note 7.

[10] *Automotive Tooling Systems v. Wilkens and Others* 2007 (2) SA 271, 279 (SCA).

[11] *Meter Systems Holdings Ltd v. Venter and Another*, *supra* note 8, at 411.

[12] VAN HEERDEN-NEETHLING, *supra* note 1, at 218.

[13] Neethling & Rutherford, *supra* note 4, at 267.

[14] *Id.*

The remainder of this report discusses questions of infringement on trade secrets as they relate to current and former employees, as well as trade competitors. It also provides a brief outline of the remedies framework in cases of breach.

II. Employees

One way a person/company can protect trade secrets from misappropriation is by incorporating confidential information clauses in employment contracts and/or by incorporating restraint of trade clauses in service contracts.[15] A restraint of trade agreement clause may incorporate the duty not to disclose trade secrets and confidential information belonging to the employer.[16] A restraint clause prevents a person from using confidential information gained through the course of his employment to the detriment of the employer.[17] An employee who breaches this duty while still employed may be dismissed for breach of an express or implied term of his employment contract or a fiduciary duty.[18] Where the disclosure comes from a former employee, legal action can also be taken (see remedies discussion below).[19]

Enforcing restraint of trade agreements and confidentiality clauses, like any other agreement, is subject to constitutional provisions that guarantee individual rights.[20] South African courts have relied on principles such as public interest as well as reasonableness, public policy, legally recognizable interest, and/or proprietary interest worthy of protection as core factors in reaching their decisions when asked to adjudicate and enforce the protection of trade secrets and know-how.[21]

A restraint clause is unenforceable if it prevents a party, after termination of his or her employment, from partaking in trade or commerce without a corresponding interest of the other party deserving protection.[22] A party who breaches a confidentiality clause or restraint of trade clause and seeks to avoid the contractual obligation to which he solemnly agreed is required to prove that the public interest would be detrimentally affected by the enforcement of the clause.[23] The courts also examine the issue of reasonableness. The requirement of reasonableness is used to assess whether the restraint of trade clause is contrary to public policy.[24] The South African Supreme Court has identified four questions in assessing the reasonableness of a restraint:

---

[15] *Reddy v. Siemens Telecommunications*, *supra* note 5, at 491–501 (SCA).

[16] *Id.*; *see also Wespro (Cape Town) v. Stephenson*, *supra* note 6, at 458–59.

[17] *Reddy v. Siemens Telecommunications*, *supra* note 5, at 491.

[18] *Wespro (Cape Town) v. Stephenson*, *supra* note 6, at 457–58.

[19] *Id.* at 454–59.

[20] S. AFR. CONST. 1996, §§ 8 & 36, http://www.info.gov.za/documents/constitution/1996/index.htm.

[21] *Reddy v. Siemens Telecommunications*, *supra* note 5, at 496–97; *Basson v. Chilwan and Others* 1993 at 49–56 (Sup. Ct. App. Div.), *available at* http://www.saflii.org/za/cases/ZASCA/1993/61.pdf.

[22] *Reddy v. Siemens Telecommunications*, *supra* note 5, at 497.

[23] *Basson v. Chilwan and Others*, *supra* note 21, at 53–54.

[24] Van Jaarsveld et al., *Labour Law*, *in* 13(1) THE LAWS OF SOUTH AFRICA 9, 113 (J.A. Faris ed., 2d ed. 2009).

(1) Does one party have an interest that deserves protection after termination of the agreement?

(2) If so, is that interest threatened by the other party?

(3) In that case, does such an interest weigh qualitatively against the interest of the other party not to be economically inactive and unproductive?

(4) Whether an aspect of public policy having nothing to do with the relationship between the parties requires that the restraint be maintained or rejected.[25]

If the interest of the party sought to be restrained outweighs the interest to be protected, the restraint will be deemed unreasonable and unenforceable.[26]

Other lower courts have expanded these questions to include whether the restraint is broader than what is necessary to protect the interest in question.[27] Recent court decisions have also considered the issue of whether the employer has a proprietary interest in the know-how acquired by an employee.[28] South African courts treat the determination of whether an employer has a proprietary interest, either generally[29] or within the know-how[30] acquired by an employee, as a question of fact.[31]

III. Competitors

The unauthorized acquisition and use of a rival's trade secret is recognized as a form of unlawful competition.[32] Competition involving wrongful interference with another's right to trade constitutes an injury and may result in an Aquilian action[33] if it results in damages.[34] In 1968, the Supreme Court of South Africa held that,

> [w]here a trader has by the exercise of his skill and labour compiled information which he distributes to his clients up on a confidential basis, . . . a rival trader who is not a client but in some manner obtains this information and, well knowing its true nature and the basis up on which it was distributed, uses it in his competing business, commits a wrongful act vis-à-vis the latter and will be liable to him in damages. In an appropriate

---

[25] *Reddy v. Siemens Telecommunications*, supra note 5, at 497.

[26] *Id.*

[27] *Nampesca (SA) Products (Pty) Ltd v. Zaderer* 1999 (20) ILJ 549, 556–57 (C), *available at* http://heinonline.org/HOL/Page?handle=hein.journals/iljuta20&div=84&g_sent=1&collection=journals (by subscription).

[28] *Automotive Tooling Systems v. Wilkens and Others*, supra note 10, at 277–79.

[29] *Nampesca (SA) Products (Pty) Ltd v. Zadeer*, supra note 27, at 562.

[30] *Automotive Tooling Systems v. Wilkens and Others*, supra note 10, at 279.

[31] *Id.*

[32] VAN HEERDEN-NEETHLING, supra note 1, at 219.

[33] An Aquilian action is a Roman law principle that enables a person who has suffered calculable damage (patrimonial loss) to seek and obtain appropriate compensation. *You and Your Rights: Aquilian Action*, LEGALITY, http://www.legalcity.net/Index.cfm?fuseaction=RIGHTS.article&ArticleID=7059794 (last visited Aug. 14, 2013).

[34] *Premier Hangers CC v. Ployoak (Pty) Ltd* 1997 (1) SA 416, 421–22 (SCA), *available at* http://www.saflii.org/za/cases/ZASCA/1996/119.html.

case, the plaintiff trader would also be entitled to claim an interdict [injunction] against the continuation of such wrongful conduct.[35]

A person commits a tort of unlawful competition "if the acquisition and use of a rival's trade secret are likely to cause the latter loss of custom, thereby in principle infringing his right to goodwill ('right to carry on his trade and attract custom')."[36]

The protection of a trade secret is not limited to its proprietors; other legal users such as licensees of the proprietor are also protected. The Witwatersrand Local Division held in a 1980 case that

> [t]he dishonest use of confidential information is a species of unlawful competition or unlawful interference with the trade of another which our laws will not countenance. The trader's remedy is Aquilian. In principle there is no reason for limiting the scope of this type of action by conferring it only up on the owner of the confidential information. The wrong up on which the remedy lies is not an invasion of rights of property. The wrong is the unlawful infringement of a competitor's right to be protected from unlawful competition. If A is in lawful possession of the confidential information of B and such possession was obtained by A to further his own business interests, it would be a wrong committed against A for C, a trade rival of A, to obtain that information by dishonest means from A for the purpose of using it the to the detriment of the business of A. That it might also be a wrong committed against B is another matter. Once there is a dishonest conduct of the type just posited and loss or damage suffered thereby to the person against whom the wrong has been committed, the requisites for Aquilian liability are present.[37]

Unlawful competition by a trade rival through unauthorized acquisition, use, and/or publication of a trade secret entitles the wronged party to an injunction and/or damages, remedies that carry different evidentiary thresholds (see the section on remedies below).[38]

IV. Remedies

Upon a finding of inappropriate use of trade secrets, South African courts have various remedies at their disposal depending on the parties involved. In an action based on unlawful competition, the wronged competitor has two remedies available: an injunction ("interdict")[39] and an Aquilian action.[40] An injunction requires a showing of unlawful conduct or a "well-founded apprehension" that unlawful conduct will be committed and the unavailability of other remedy/ies to the claimant.[41] It also applies when there is fear/expectation that the infringement

---

[35] *Dun and Bradstreet (Pty) Ltd v. S.A. Merchants Combined Credit Bureau (Cape) Ltd*, 1968 (1) SA 209, 221 (C).

[36] VAN HEERDEN-NEETHLING, *supra* note 1, at 221.

[37] *Prok Africa (Pty) Ltd and Another v. NTH (Pty) Ltd and Others* 1980 (3) SA 687, 687–88 (W).

[38] VAN HEERDEN-NEETHLING, *supra* note 1, at 221–22.

[39] *Reddy v. Siemens Telecommunications*, *supra* note 5, at 486.

[40] VAN HEERDEN-NEETHLING, *supra* note 1, at 221.

[41] *Id.*; H. DANIELS, BECK'S THEORY AND PRINCIPLES OF PLEADING IN CIVIL ACTIONS 329 (6th ed. 2002).

is actually or potentially recurrent.[42] An Aquilian action requires proof of damages and causation.[43]

In an action based on an inappropriate use of trade secrets by persons bound by a contract or a fiduciary responsibility (such as an agent or employee), the wronged party has a number of remedies at his disposal. In this instance, he may bring an action for the breach of an express or implied contractual term.[44] A remedy in tort may also be sought.[45]

When the action for breach involves a former employee, the process gets slightly complicated. This is due to the recognition of two forms of confidential information: trade secrets, and other confidential information that enjoys protection.[46] The former is information so secret that it may not be used by an employee in competition with the former employer during or after the termination of employment, while the latter is confidential information that remains in the employee's memory after the termination of the employment contract and forms part of his skill that may be used even to compete with a former employer.[47] Thus, an allegation of a breach against a former employee would involve a determination as to whether the information involved is a trade secret or other confidential information. If the information is indeed a trade secret, the former employer may seek an injunction and/or damages.[48]

Specifically, to successfully obtain an injunction or damages, be it against a trade rival or a current or former employee, a claimant needs to prove that

- he has an interest in the information (not necessarily ownership),

- the information is confidential in nature (specifically a trade secret if the defendant is a former employee),

- there is a relationship between the parties from which a duty arises on the part of the defendant to preserve the information (this could be an employment relationship or a situation where the parties are trade rivals and the defendant obtained the information in question improperly),

- the defendant made improper use of the information, and

- the claimant suffered damages as a result (this is applicable only when seeking damages).[49]

---

[42] *Strike Productions (Pty) Ltd v. Bon View Trading 131 (Pty) Ltd and Others*, *supra* note 7.

[43] *Id.*

[44] *Id.*

[45] VAN HEERDEN-NEETHLING, *supra* note 1, at 224.

[46] *Waste Products Utilization (Pty) Ltd v. Wilkes and Another* 2003 (2) SA 515, 518 (WLD).

[47] *Id.*

[48] *Id.*

[49] *Waste Products Utilization (Pty) Ltd v. Wilkes and Another*, *supra* note 46, at 518–19 (WLD); *Strike Productions (Pty) Ltd v. Bon View Trading 131 (Pty) Ltd and Others*, *supra* note 7.